How to Have
Whatever You Want

PAUL SHIPLEY

ISBN:1539347052
ISBN-13: 978-1539347057

DEDICATION

This book is dedicated to all of the people who are striving for a better life, those who know that they have something great within them, a reason for being here in the first place.

CONTENTS

ACKNOWLEDGMENTS

Over the past many years I have attended seminars, read books and listened to many hours of tapes by some of the world's greatest teachers and philosophers. I have learned a lot from those people and they are too many to mention by name however I humbly acknowledge their contribution to my education.

1 HOW?

How to have whatever you want! A big statement coming from anyone, let alone me. But here's the truth of it, anyone can have whatever they want if a few simple elements are all aligned properly.

Let's start at the beginning, and I know that this might sound obvious to many but the one and only place to start is to figure out exactly what it is that you want. Whenever I ask people the question, 'what do you want the most?' I usually get one of 3 answers,

1 – MONEY,
2 – HEALTH,
3 – HAPPINESS.

Sounds fair enough to me, and all of these things fit perfectly with a humans basic needs, to be safe, cared for and contented.

My next question to you would be, what is it, precisely, about having money or health or happiness that you want? What is the main difference that having that thing will make in your life? How will it make you a better person? Or does it just sound like a nice thing to have?

Let me explain, I used to think that I wanted money and I chased it relentlessly, by sheer determination, some good fortune and very little skill I managed to acquire money and many of the trappings that went along with it BUT I couldn't hold on to it. And here's one thing that I did learn, money can disappear a lot faster than you can accumulate it.

Time and time again I chased after money, headed to the top, or so I believed, only to slide right back down the hill again. Why? Because I didn't understand what it was that I truly believed having the money would give me. All I could see was the cash, I had no idea that the cash is not the goal, the money is not the end product, neither is the car, the house, the boat, the holiday home, the world travel.

These are all very nice things, don't get me wrong, and I have enjoyed having them, but they are not the answer to my dream. I used to think that they were, in fact I completely believed that they were, but if that was true then how come they are so easy to lose? How come the 'things' come and go again?

What I am driving at is that, for me personally, what I wanted most in life was not what I believed it to be and I wasted a big chunk of my life aiming at the wrong target. All of that time and effort are gone, I can't get them back, in life you do not get to start over at the beginning – you can only start again from where you are today. Time is precious, don't waste it, even by accident, and make every day count.

This is the hardest thing you will ever have to do, figure out what it is that you truly want out of life, once you have this part nailed down then the rest is easy. 'But what if something happens that changes my priorities?' I hear you ask. Well that's just fine as long as you spot the change quickly and alter your focus accordingly. So long as you are paying attention to your life, living it to the fullest in the pursuit of your dream, changing direction is no problem.

Let me give you a few pointers here. Let's say that your answer to my first question was 'happiness.' OK write down the word, happiness, at the top of a sheet of paper. Now think of the happiest moments in your life so far, write them down, include details of who else was there, where it was, what made it special, really get to the bottom of WHY that made you happy. Now we start to see what circumstances, what events, what type of people, what type of place form the ingredients to your happiness.

Focus on the details, the secrets are in the fine print, even things such as the time of day or what clothes you were wearing could be vital. Miss nothing out. What you should finish up with is your own, unique recipe for happiness, your next move is to work out how to bring those ingredients together whenever you want to. Don't forget, like all good recipes, you are able to tweak the ingredients as you go along, even try something completely different, add an extra flavour (maybe a new person) to the mix. You will always be in control of your own kitchen. Being happy can happen by chance but you can also take control of the circumstances that lead to you being happy.

Now what if someone says happiness because they have never experienced true happiness, only witnessed it in others? How does that person get to have a unique recipe for happiness?

In fact the same could be said about someone who answered money but never had any, or answers health because their health has always been poor? Are these people doomed? Not at all, I will get to that in just a moment.

Here is another tip, something that is worth knowing right from the get – go, whatever happened in your past does not have to define your future.

What do I mean by that? Well, I come from a very humble background, as a baby my first home was in a bedsit over a fish and chip shop, my first crib was an empty drawer from the chest of drawers that came with the furnished bedsit. Luckily for me my mother had so few clothes that she didn't need more than one drawer to keep them in. My first baby bedding was a folded towel and a bedsheet.

Aged 2, when my brother came along, we moved to a two bedroomed terraced house. The view out front was of the terraced houses across the street and the view out back was of the communal back-yard and the block of outside toilets. There was no indoor bathroom, we bathed in a tin bath on the living room floor and, even in the dead of winter, freezing conditions, snow and rain, and we put on our coats, hats and boots to go out to the lavatory. For the next 16 years 5 children plus mom and dad lived contentedly in that house until, aged 18, I moved out to get married and start my own journey. Aged 16 I had left school with no qualification because it was expected of me to go to work and help to support my family, so that's what I did.

I remember, just before leaving school, we each had a meeting with someone called a 'Career Advice Officer.' This was the person who assessed your academic achievements and reports from your tutors and then, based on his judgement and wisdom, he pointed you towards your most suitable career path.

Now I knew that it wouldn't take him long to review my academic achievements because I didn't have any, and I also knew that most of the reports from my tutors were going to say something about my very many absences from class. I had a terrible attendance record on account of spending a lot of my school time at home helping mom with the other, younger kids.

What this guy said to me that day has always stuck with me, he said, 'Paul, you will never amount to much and so far as I can tell you have no skills and no talent. But that's OK because the world will always need people to do the lowly jobs that no one else wants so my advice to you is to take whatever job comes along and hope for the best.'

I can tell you now, I was not inspired. I did not walk away with a spring in my step ready to embrace the future. I was terrified, filled with self-doubt and already struggling with the beginnings of what would become a life long battle with mental health. The world looked very big and very mean so I cast my eyes downwards and for years I never even looked at the future, let alone imagined one where I could become anything more than what I was told I would be.

So, in my mind, going from where I started to where I am now I can honestly tell you that your background, the things in your past, do not have to determine who or where you will be in the future. So don't go around blaming you poor education, poor upbringing, past mistakes or whatever. Learn whatever lessons you can and put all of the rest of it behind you.

Next important thing is, DON'T LOOK BACK! Keep your eyes and your mind focused on the direction you want to go. If you are constantly looking back then you will end up right where you started. You will have what you are focusing on so if you focus on past mistakes you will get the same mistakes all over again. Don't do it, you've been there already and you didn't like it the last time so why go there again?

So, how do you create a recipe for having something that you never had before? How do you know what it truly feels like to have that thing? How do you even know for sure that the thing you long for is, in actual fact, the think that you want the most? And how do you know that having it will bring you the desired or expected effects?

A guy say's. 'Well just let me have the money for a while and then I will tell you if I was right or not' which is fair enough but just think about all of that wasted time and effort if you are wrong!

Now it's not my job to tell you what you should or should not aspire to, what you should go after with all of your heart and strength. No, not at all, what I am saying is that it is wise to be as sure as possible before putting in all of that effort. As I said earlier, I know what it is like to make that mistake, to get caught up in a quest for the wrong thing and believe me, the price of that quest was high, very high.

Let me ask you this, if you could choose to leave behind a legacy of some sort, something that people would remember you for, something that would instantly link your name to it, what would that something be? Or to be fair, what SORT of something would it be?

Would you want to be remembered as the sort of person who was always there for others when they needed help or needed a friend? The sort of person who gave to charity? The sort of person who flashed his cash around all the time? A wonderful parent? A fantastic spouse or partner? In fact, can you think of anyone right now who is already the sort of person that you want to be remembered as?

That is a great place to start. It's called 'Having a life's purpose' a reason for doing things, a reason for being here in the first place. For some people that looks like being the person who found a certain cure, or discovered a new route up a mountain, or won a gold medal at the Olympics, or devoted themselves to helping the needy of the world. If you can find your life's purpose, your reason why, then you are already ahead of the game and I believe that nothing can stop you from fulfilling that dream.

Your life's purpose may never lead to fame or fortune in the popular sense of the word but how might it make you feel? When you come to the end of life's journey how amazing would it be to look back and say, 'I did that.' 'I didn't just pass through this world being average, I made a difference.'

I believe that every one of us was put here for a reason, that if we have dreams then we were given those dreams for a reason and it is our duty to follow them. A great man once declared, 'I have a dream.' And what did he do about his dream? He told everyone what the dream was and then he spent the rest of his life working to make that dream a reality. I don't think that he ever sat down and thought, I want to be famous and this is how I can achieve it. No, he knew exactly what his life's purpose was and as a side effect of working on that purpose he became one of history's best known characters.

Now your life's purpose doesn't have to be world changing or affect millions of other people. It might be something totally personal or limited to your own immediate family. That's just as good, as long as it fulfills your true desire, the thing that you want to become.

Let's assume then that you have identified your true desire, your life's purpose, your 'WHY'. How do you get from where you are now to where you want to be? For each of us the path will be different, simply because we are all different in the first place and we all start out from a different place. Wherever you are starting from there are some basic, simple steps that all successful people take and we can do the same.

2 STEP ONE

The first step is to boil down your 'WHY' into a brief statement, for example, 'I am a happy and contented person.' Or maybe, 'I enjoy good health and a great quality of life.' How about, 'I have all the money I could ever need.' It could be, 'I have helped my family out of poverty.' 'I sent my children to college.' 'I am a successful author.'

Remember, your 'why' is the person that you want to become, the person that you want to be remembered as.

We don't need to include the reasons for wanting it or any of the peripheral things that will come to you when you do become that person. All of those things are already clear in our minds and they will be ours automatically when we achieve our core desire, our 'why'.

For example, the car, the house, the financial security etc. will automatically be ours when we can truly say, 'I have all the money I could ever need.'

This is step one for a good reason, it will become the foundation stone on which you will build your future. If we don't get this right, don't make it strong, solid and dependable then how can we expect it to support us?

How will it stand a chance of holding us upright when the strong winds of life come along to batter us? Trust me, you will be battered from time to time, you will be tested and tried. We will get tired, weary and struggle but our foundation stone, our 'WHY' will keep us solid.

Think about this as well, if it doesn't support us and give us the strength to carry on when things are tough then is it really the thing we want the most or is it just something that sounds like a good idea at the time?

Remember the old story of the two men? One of them built his house on a foundation of rock, the other on a foundation of sand. When the stormy weather came the house built on sand was destroyed but the other one, built on rock, stood firm.

It is vital that this statement includes the following;

A, It must be positive

B, It must be in the present tense

C, It must assume that you have achieved your purpose.

.

3 STEP TWO

Write down your statement on a small card and put it in your wallet.

By keeping the statement in your wallet you are doing several significant things. You are associating the value of the statement with the value of your cash and your cards.

This is a very important psychological move, just think how upset you would be if you lost your wallet. Have you ever had a time when you couldn't find your wallet? Do you remember the rising sense of panic, the stress, the worry in case it was completely lost or stolen?

You are placing your statement in one of the few places that, usually, only you will look, a very private place. This element of privacy reinforces the very personal and deeply cared for nature of the statement.

You are carrying it with you everywhere, on business, at work, to the store, during your leisure activities etc. Your wallet is one of the things that you will rarely be without. People often check, subconsciously, that their wallet is still where it should be, still safe, still with them, by, in the case of men, touching the pocket where it is kept.

Whenever we look in our wallet we will see our own statement and, subconsciously, it will be refreshed in our minds. We don't necessarily have to read the statement every time we see it, we already know what it says, what it means to us and how important it is. If we really put our heart and soul into writing down the statement then the words will be projected by our 'Mind's Eye'.

At the same time all of the other things associated with being in the wallet will be re-affirmed, the value, the special privacy, the importance, the safety, the security of being in our wallet.

All of these elements are an intrinsic part of the almost spiritual quality of belonging inside a wallet. You have a wallet anyway so why not have it work for you?

4 STEP THREE

Write it down every day as the first entry into your diary.

It goes in that space you usually leave blank before your first meeting or appointment, you know, the time you allow yourself for drinking coffee, checking email and stuff like that.

When we do this each day becomes a day focused on achieving that goal.

Our every action, every thought, every word will be pre-loaded with the power of our most important goal, our 'Why.'

In a way we are setting about a kind of 'self-brainwashing' although I prefer to think of it as a process of re-wiring the mind. We already know that, after a fairly short time, a repeated action or thought will become a habit. A habit is something that we do automatically or without conscious effort like breathing in and out.

Let me ask you a question, what is the 'default status' of your mind? What I mean is, when you have nothing specific to occupy your thoughts where does your mind go automatically?

Does it wander about all over the place, flitting from one idea to the next? Do you get to thinking about past mistakes, longing for 'the good old days'? Are you, what some might call, away with the fairies? Spaced out? Just drifting?

Don't panic if you answer yes to any of the above, the vast majority of people will also answer yes, in fact the average person finds themselves in this state many times a day. But that's the problem isn't it? We have already decided that we don't want to be average.

We want to be exceptional and let me tell you where an exceptional person's mind goes when they have down time. It goes to living the life that they are striving towards. They have re-set their default status to automatically focus on a mental picture of what their life will be like when they have achieved their WHY.

They have built such a realistic vision for themselves that they can not only see it, they can feel it, smell it, hear it and taste the sweet taste of success. And I want that to be true for you. I want you to have such a vision, a vision so powerful that it becomes like a magnet that can draw you towards it. An automatic state of being that only exceptional people enjoy.

How do you build such a thing? It takes time and practice and patience but by keeping your statement in the front of your minds every day then that statement will become a habit. A way of thinking about yourself that is automatic and your imagination will help you to build the rest of the image.

The sounds, the feel, the smell and the taste of it can all be found in your mind, you only have to look hard enough.

Have a go right now, take a few minutes for yourself and visualize having achieved your life's purpose. How proud will you feel? How happy are you with the results? How do other people think of you and what do they say about you?

Close your eyes and imagine yourself as you will be on the day that you can say to the world, 'I did that' 'I made that happen' 'I have done all that I was put here to do'.

What a day that will be, what a feeling when you have achieved the very pinnacle of your dreams. There is nothing like the view from the top!

5 STEP FOUR

Speak it out loud as often as possible every day, (I do this first thing every morning and last thing before I go to sleep at night and whenever I can in-between).

This is going to keep you focused on your true objective both consciously and subconsciously.

When your subconscious mind is focused on something it fine tunes every move you make, every decision you take so that you always move towards you goal.

When you have the power of the subconscious mind working for you something magical happens and you will begin to find yourself in situations, in conversations and in places that move you forward towards you goal. You may not even be aware of it at the time but all of those small events will build and build until you suddenly realise that you appear to have taken a big step forward.

That big step forward wasn't a fluke, it didn't just happen by chance, it happened because you, through your subconscious mind, continually looked for ways to move you forward, one tiny step at a time.

Now, what does this tell us? First off it tells us that every little step in the right direction counts. It also tells us that many of the steps that we make will be TINY! We may not even notice that we have moved forward at all until, WHAM, we feel as though we have taken a giant leap towards our goal!

This also means that we will only ever see the giant leap if we keep up the process that helps us to make the tiny steps. We don't have to worry about the size of each step, or even try to spot them as we go along, just be ready to celebrate when we have the WHAM moment!

I won't pretend to understand the science behind this, all I can do is to ask you to have faith and let it happen.

Now don't forget that the opposite will also be true. If you have the subconscious mind focused on negative things, on reasons why you can't succeed then you will also be proved right.

I know that a lot of people teach that focusing on the positive is all that you need to do but I don't think so. Negative stuff is like weeds in a garden, they are everywhere and if the guy turns his back and says 'There are no weeds, I have a perfect garden, there are no weeds I have a perfect garden,' what's going to happen while he is not looking? Right, the weeds will be growing tall and strong behind his back!

What does this mean for us? It means that we have to keep an eye open for the weeds! Those sneaky negative thoughts that try to creep into our mind, those negative ideas that are planted by other people. Watch out for them and, just like a weed, pull them up by the root and throw them out of your mind.

Just like keeping a perfect garden, if you want to remain on track you have to do a little work as you go along.

This might be a good time to have a look at what work might be required of us? Well we are talking about some mental weeding. Pulling out all of those thoughts, ideas and suggestions that detract from our purpose. To put it bluntly if you are a vegetarian then you are not likely to be caught reading a book of meat recipes are you? What would be the point?

Similarly it would be fair to ask why people invest such a lot of time and effort in activities that do not move them towards their goal. Don't get me wrong, distractions are natural, they are everywhere (just like weeds), but even your average gardener doesn't waste his time cultivating the weeds, watering and feeding them does he? No, no, no, he put his efforts into caring for the plants that he wants to see there in the garden.

The weeds are also plants, just the wrong ones. If you made a living from producing nettle tea then you would cultivate nettles and dig out the flowering plants. The trick here is to identify the thoughts, ideas, suggestions etc. that fit with your goals and cultivate those ones. Root out the stuff you don't need, it will just be occupying important space in your mind, soaking up energy and keeping you from cultivating the right stuff!

But, you might say, 'I don't have time for all that effort, I'm busy, I have a job, a family and commitments to meet. It takes all of my time just to keep going, I go to work, watch a little TV and go to bed. When am I supposed to do this extra weeding?'

My answer to you is this, everyone has only 24 hours given to them each day and everyone is allowed to choose how they spend those hours, if you are serious about achieving your life's dreams, your goals, your life purpose then you have got to prioritize.

By that I mean, if watching the TV is more important to you than your life's purpose then go ahead and watch the TV, it's up to you.

6 STEP FIVE

I heard a mother talking to her child recently, she was saying something along the lines of, 'I don't want you hanging around with those kids any more. Those kids are losers and I don't want you to end up like them.'

I'm sure that we have all heard people say similar things over the years and, like many other common expressions, it is founded in truth.

Research has proven that, over time, a person's actions or behavior will automatically tune into that of the people around them. They will begin to think alike, to share ideals and beliefs without question. The even begin to sound alike, to have the same accent and use the same words and phrases.

This phenomenon is based in our human desire to be accepted, to be part of a group and not to stand out because standing out or being different could leave us out on our own. An animal on its own becomes an easy target for predators, an animal in a group feels safe. We don't use the expression, 'safety in numbers' by accident but because it is true. Humans in general work best when part of a group. In fact it is quite natural to fear being alone or to fear loneliness.

True, there are some people who seem to thrive on being alone but in truth very very few of us, in our heat of hearts, prefer to be alone all of the time.

Here is the brief version of a recent social experiment which proves the point. In a waiting room a small number of actors sat mingled with the regular clients.

Whenever a bell rang the actors stood up for a moment and then sat down again. After several rings of the bell the regular clients began to join in and stand up for a moment.

One by one the actors left the room but each time the bell rang the remaining people stood up. As new clients arrived and joined the group they would also stand with the others every time the bell rang.

The actors were long gone but the behavior continued, why? Because it had now become the normal thing to do in that place, afterwards when people were asked, 'why did you stand up?' they answered, 'Because everyone else did so I thought I should also do it.'

Now here's a thought. If hanging around with losers might make me a loser as well, what could happen if I was hanging around with successful people? If I was hanging out with champions, with people who achieved great things, people who were already the sort of person that I aspired to be?

The moral of step five is, be careful who you spend your time with. If you wanted to be a great surgeon you wouldn't ask a tailor to teach you would you? Both of these guys know how to sew but only one of them has the skills that you need to learn.

7 STEP SIX

How can we make this knowledge work for us?

Well, how about identifying some people who are already the sort of person that we want to become and hanging out with them as much as possible?

OK I know that this might not sound practical and I don't want you to turn into some kind of a creepy stalker, following folks around and taking notes! How about this then. How easy is it to find out about people using the internet these days? Very easy. How many great achievers have written books, published articles, given interviews? Just about all of them.

With all of the information available to us today we can find out exactly what makes a successful person tick, read their story, research their background, follow in their footsteps and spend quality time with them all from the comfort of our own home.

But the guy says, 'I'm busy, you know I have to go to work, spend time with my family, have my dinner, watch a little TV and then get to bed. I don't have time for all of this research, study and reading!'

Trust me, if that's your attitude, if that's how much you care about yourself, your family and your future then maybe you need to think again about finding your life purpose.

Let's say that your heart's desire is to be a great writer. Are there any other writers out there in the world who are already great? Plenty of them. Do you have a chance of becoming friends with them and spending time with them in person? No? Didn't think so.

Is it possible for you to read the things they have written? Could you find any reviews about that work done by experts? Could you find copies of any interviews they have given to the press, TV or radio? Would that information give you some clues as to why they are great writers, what it is that makes their work so special?

To be honest, you can probably find out where they were born, what schools they went to, how well they did in class, who their friends are, who their spouse is, what pets hey like and where they went last year on vacation!

We are living in an extraordinary time. A time when there is so much information at our fingertips that it is almost overwhelming. You can ask Google literally anything and have answers instantly.

I bet that you can find out things about a successful person that even their best friends don't know. Which means that you don't have to be physically in the company of someone to learn from them.

It's up to you. Would you rather spend your time hanging around with average people and know that you will finish up just the same, an average person? Or would you rather get to working on your dream? Spending time learning from successful people by hanging around with information about them?

What's the worst that could happen? Well maybe you learn a few things and become one of the successful people yourself! It has to be worth the risk because we already know what the alternative is and we don't want to be average!

Let me tell you about a well-known mountain climber. He looked at a mountain one day and said, 'I am going to stand at the top of this mountain.'

His friends and colleagues all said he must be mad. No-one had ever made it the top before, the one approach was too steep and deadly, the other approach was too slippery and icy. They told him, 'There is no way, it can't be done.'

Now this mountaineer had already decided that it was his life's purpose to conquer this mountain, to find a route to the top where there had never been a route found before. To achieve the impossible climb and show the way to others who would follow in his footsteps.

He turned to all his friends and critics and said,

"Look, I am going to do it, there will be a way and I will find it. There is no way that this mountain is going to beat me. Once I set out keep your eyes on me because you will either see me waving from the top of lying dead on the side."

Needless to say Edmund Hillary made it to the top of Everest and a great many more have followed in his footsteps.

The real key is in the degree of determination, the self-belief, the personal commitment that drove him on though the preparations, the training, before he even got to the mountain.

You too can be just like that. You too can achieve whatever you want to. Even if it has never been done before, if no-one believes it possible, if the experts think you are crazy to even try. You do not have to believe that the world of achievement is just for someone else because it's not. The world is yours for the taking so grab a handful right now.

8 COMPOUND IT

It's not new and it's not rocket science but like a lot of good ideas it doesn't hurt to have another look at them from time to time.

The Compound Effect, how can it benefit you? How can you make it work for you, even when you aren't paying attention to it?

Let's back up a little, just in case we are not entirely sure, what is the compound effect? It is the total effect, over time, of small events, choices, actions or thoughts.

What does that mean? If you trade your apple for a chocolate bar today will you gain 10 pounds? No, probably not, if you trade your apple for chocolate every day for the next 90 days will you gain 10 pounds? Probably, carry on for a year and you will gain? Lots of pounds!

OK let's try that again with a more positive action, if you contact 10 new prospects today will your business grow much? Probably not, how about if you contacted 10 new prospect a day for 90 days, would you see some return? Almost certainly and 10 is not a very big number in isolation however compounded over time it can become substantial.

What I am saying is that what appear to small changes, actions events or even thoughts, by repeating them, certain things will happen automatically.

First, after around 30 days the event becomes a habit and when that happens your brain puts it into the 'Auto-Pilot' department, in other words you no longer even have to make a conscious effort, you just do it. All our lives we convert actions into habits without even realizing it. Do you know someone who always uses certain expressions? Perhaps they call people sir, or mate, or bud, or (in some areas) even duck?

The hardest part of giving up smoking is not getting the nicotine out of your body, that happens relatively quickly, the hardest part is breaking the habit of smoking. When you would usually have a cigarette, say after a meal, your brain automatically triggers the habit sequence to get you to light up! It's a powerful thing, the human mind, but it can be trained, re-wired, but the training takes time. The required length of time varies from person to person, some can re-wire quickly but most people take around 90 days to establish a new habit.

Next the universal law of averages comes into play, which means that you will start to see results (positive or negative) automatically. This also means that we should not expect the results to be favorable all of the time. Just like flipping a coin, sometimes it comes down heads, but not every time.

The law of averages makes sure that, given enough tries, the results will be even at the end of the day. How is that helpful? Well, it's better to have a realistic expectation before putting in the effort. After all, if I convinced you that flipping the coin in a certain way would guarantee coming down heads every time how will you feel when the law of averages steps in and gives you tails instead of heads?

So now we know that it would be madness to expect to win every single time we won't be despondent and quit the first time that we get it wrong. The key is to keep on flipping the coin because it simply has to land on heads at least half of the time.

Finally the law of momentum will propel you in that direction with less and less effort from you, automatically. Just like pushing a motorcar, if you have ever had to do this then you will know how much effort is needed just to get the thing moving in the first place. But what happens once you have some movement? Keeping it moving is so much easier than getting started. You move from the hard work of creating momentum to the relatively easy task of just keeping things rolling along.

Don't forget, the compound effect works just as well with negative, bad habits as it does with good ones, it is an effect - it can't tell the difference!

Are small changes easy to make - absolutely, in fact we spend so much time sweating over the big choices that we tend to ignore the small stuff and it's the small stuff that can make all of the difference - over time.

Are small changes easy NOT to make, of course, that's why the majority of people don't make them. And by the way are the majority of people successful or just average?

That's right, the majority are just average, so there is the answer – right there – the best way to not be average is to **not do** what the average person keeps on doing.

9 GRATITUDE

I firmly believe in the law of gratitude and several other people have written about this subject in great depth.

Would it be OK with you if I gave you a quick overview, a taste as it were, of this amazing law of nature?

We need to start by being aware of, or reminded of, a few basic things. First of all everything in our universe is made up of tiny particles called atoms, as far as I can find out the same atoms have been around forever and those same atoms will continue to be around long after we are gone.

Basically, the universe is the ultimate at recycling, re-using the same particles over and over again to make different things. For example, an animal dies, its body decomposes into the ground and becomes part of the earth which becomes the food for a growing tree. Over time, the animal has effectively become a tree, or a part of the tree because the particles which were the animal don't go away, they simply change into another state of being.

So what does that tell us? It tells us that the universe is made up of a limited amount of stuff, it also tells us that the universe is able to re-use that stuff in whatever way appears to be best at the time.

Another thing we learn is that the universe is not discriminating, it treats all particles in the same way, it re-uses them. Some of the things those particles become are highly useful to humans, some of the things are deadly. Sometimes we take the useful stuff and turn it into something deadly and sometimes we take the deadly stuff and turn it into medicine.

What has all of this got to do with the law of gratitude? Simply this, everything we could ever want is already out there in the world and as it gets used up, the universe can make some more. Some things obviously take longer to make than others but even so, they can be made and remade over and over again.

The only thing we need to know is, 'How do I get my hands on the things that I need and want?'

The answer to that question was written down for us a long time ago in a great many places. Most people will be familiar with a book called The Bible, yes? In this book we are told, 'ASK, and it will be given to you.'

It doesn't say 'Take from someone else' or 'Moan and groan about your lack of it' or even 'Hope for, or Wish for' It simply says, "ASK".

So what does 'ASK' mean? Are we just going to sit around saying, 'I want, I want, I want'? Probably not. This is where gratitude comes into play.

I am going to suggest something that you might think a little odd but trust me, this is the very BEST way to ASK.

Express you heartfelt gratitude for the thing you would like to receive! I know, it sounds strange to be saying 'thank you' for something that you don't have yet but bear with me for a few more minutes and I think that you will see the logic.

First of all, think of five or six things that you are currently grateful for, it doesn't have to be anything huge, start with the basic things. Here are a few pointers, do you have food to eat? A home? Clothes to wear? Family? Friends?

Get the idea? We can be grateful for all of the ordinary everyday things that we usually take for granted. Now, add on to the end of your list your hearts' desire.

Your list might go something like this;

I am truly grateful for the meal I had today,
I am truly grateful for the home that I live in
I am truly grateful for the clothes that I am wearing
I am truly grateful for my loving family

I am truly grateful for my wonderful friends
I am truly grateful for becoming a successful writer.

Now let's just think back to our earlier comments about re-wiring our sub-conscious mind. Can you see how, by associating the thing we want the most, but don't yet have, with the things that we do have AND being grateful for it, we bring that thing into the present? It is no longer something in the distant future, it's here, right now.

It is very important to express your gratitude in a genuine, heartfelt way. Don't rush it, don't fake it, don't pay lip-service, make it real. Learn to feel true gratitude for all of the things you have right now and that same deep feeling will be applied to your ASKING at the end.

A number of amazing things will happen, firstly you will start to look around your current world to find more and more things to be grateful for in the present. Next, when you focus such positive emotion on a thing you automatically attract more of the same. (This element also applies to negative emotion so if you constantly complain about your lack of something then you will continue to get the same lack of it). Your emotional state will, in a way, radiate around you and not only affect you and your own actions but it will also affect the people around you, their actions, thoughts and feelings will become tuned in to your own.

The proof of this is easy to see. Have you ever known anyone who was mostly miserable and complaining? How did the people around them react? Were they full of joy and positive thoughts, or were they brought down to the same low level as the complainer? On the other hand, do you know anyone who is always smiling and jolly? How do the people around that person respond? Am I right or am I right?

So if our grateful, positive energy is going to attract to us more of the things we are grateful for could the same rule apply to being grateful for the thing we don't even have yet?

Of Course! The laws of the universe don't know that we don't yet have it, all they know is that our grateful, positive energy is genuine and let it attract to us what? Right, MORE of the same things. The universe can turn its supply of particles into anything at all so you might as well go ahead and place your order today.

Call me crazy if you like but what have you got to lose?

10 KARMA

Karma is a way of talking about cause and effect. The spiritual qualities of Karma have long been accepted at the very heart of ancient religions such as Hinduism and Buddhism.

What is Karma all about then, and can we put it to work for us in our journey towards our goals?

Well one way of describing Karma is simply, 'What you sow is what you will reap.' In other words, if you want to reap corn then don't be sowing barley!

This also means that even the stuff that we sow accidentally will bear fruit so we need to be careful about what exactly we go around sowing.

In some cultures the expression, 'what goes around comes around' is a popular way of describing Karma and I heard it used in a story just recently.

A Lady was about to maneuver into a parking space one morning when a young man nipped around her and took the space. She gave him a honk on her hooter to show her annoyance, the man turned to her and called her various abusive names before walking away.

Around 30 minutes later the man was called into a meeting room to have his interview for a great job. He was confident that his qualifications and good references would get him a job offer so he walked briskly through the door only to stop dead in his tracks. There, on the other side of the meeting room table and clearly in charge of the interview panel sat the very woman he had insulted in the car park.

His chances of a job offer plummeted to zero because what goes around, comes around.

He had accidentally sown a whole bunch of ill feeling and animosity in the car park and, in this instance, it bore fruit very quickly.

Let's think about cause and effect for a moment. The theory says that for every action there is an equal and opposite reaction, in the case of the story above, one person acted with hostility and therefore received hostility. What he gave out came back towards him. If he had not taken the parking space but helped the woman by guiding her into it what a difference that would have made to his day! By giving out kindness and caring he would have received kindness and caring (and possibly a new job as well).

The good news about Karma is, it's just a law, it has no feelings one way or the other, like gravity it just happens This means that we can take control over what we receive from Karma, simply by sowing the right seeds we know that the natural law of Karma (you reap what you sow) will give us the right crop.

To nail this down even tighter I can't help but notice how Karma has similarities with the law of gratitude, in that case we are being truly grateful for something that we don't yet have so that the universe (nature) will give us some more of it. It's very similar to sowing seeds, very accurate and specific seeds in that case.

So how are we going to take control of Karma and have it work for us? Well, we can start by testing it on small things at first such as treating everyone we meet with a friendly positive attitude. Make a point of treating people in the way that we want people to treat us and see what happens.

If we drive then why not put the same theory to the test with our driving habits? When we are out and about we could hold a door open for someone, give up our seat for someone, and practice having a cheerful look on our face. Be grateful and say thank you whenever we can.

After a while the conscious effort we make to do these things will become, you guessed it, a habit. We will do them automatically because the basic law of nature will re-wire our subconscious mind to keep on doing it.

So here we are, sowing seeds of goodwill, generosity, caring, positivity, cheerfulness and so on. When Karma starts to feed all of that back to us then WOW, we will be on easy street!

Here is another interesting thing about sowing seeds. When a farmer sows his seeds does he get back more crops than the seeds he has sown or does he get back just the same quantity?

He gets back MORE, a lot more. Otherwise there would be no point in sowing the seeds in the first place. If he only got back the same number as he planted then he might as well save himself the time and effort and keep the seeds he already has!

I don't know about you but I kind of like the idea that by using the natural laws of cause and effect (Karma) I can get back loads more of everything that I give out. And even better, nature will help me along by making my 'seed sowing' a habit that I do automatically so there will be no effort involved after a short time!

Hang on a minute, that sounds a bit like the law of momentum as well!

Some people refer to the Karma effect as 'Paying it forward' which is a great way of thinking about it. To highlight the power of paying it forward here is a true story, you may have heard it before, but this is it told by me.

One afternoon a young man was walking in the woods near to his home when he heard someone calling out for help.

Curious about the cause of the persons alarm he went through the trees to find another young man trapped in a wet, boggy mud hole. The more this chap struggled, the deeper he sank and it was obvious that he would soon drown.

Our young man, at quite some risk to himself, managed to drag the chap out from the mud and he then helped him walk to his home. When they arrived it was obvious that the chap came from a wealthy family, and the chap's father was so happy that his son had been saved that he offered our young man a cash reward. He was tempted to accept because his own circumstances were not very good, however he refused the reward saying that he had only done what any decent person would have done.

Some years later the wealthy young man became a successful doctor, his name was Louis Pasteur, and he discovered the wonderful antibiotic called penicillin.

Our young man entered the army as a soldier and was badly wounded in battle. His wound became infected and the medics feared that the infection would kill him. They decided to try out a new medicine called penicillin and, amazingly, it worked so well that he made a full recovery. His name, by the way, was Winston Churchill, who became a famous Prime Minister of England and led the Allies to victory.

It's time for me to leave you to continue your journey in your own way. I hope and pray that you have found something of value in this short book and that your life will be richer in every way.

You truly can have, whatever you want.

ABOUT THE AUTHOR

Paul is what some might call a 'Serial Entrepreneur' having been involved in a number of start-ups over the years. He has also worked as a charity volunteer and as an international life coach and mentor, helping numerous people across India and the African continent to achieve their own goals and to live a better life.

Paul is available for public speaking engagements and for one to one coaching.

www.ingramcontent.com/pod-product-compliance
Lightning Source LLC
Chambersburg PA
CBHW070240290526
45789CB00004B/1707